Climbing out of the

credit pit.

By

Chuck Baker

Table of Contents

Dedication

This book is dedicated to my wife
Cindy. For all her love and
support over the years,

Introduction

This book is going to show you how I went from a non-existent credit score to one of over 700.

I will take you step by step through the process and If you will follow what is put down in this book, you too can climb out of the credit pit.

I do have to caution you before we begin that this is a long process and will require you to make some investments in yourself and your future.

So, before you even begin you will need to be employed in at least a part time job. But full time would be ideal. And it is also a good idea that you know how to budget your money.

If you already have credit but have reached your credit limit this book will give you a guide line to follow to pay down your credit cards and reduce your debt.

So let's get started.

Step one:
The credit reports.

It is essential that you know what is in your credit reports. But many people have never even seen their credit reports let alone know what is in them.

Why is your credit report important? There might be errors on your credit reports or you could already be a victim of identity theft and not even know it. And negative entries in your credit report could even prevent you from getting or keeping a job.

Case in point, A woman was hired at a local convenience store as a clerk and the store did a background check on her which included copies of her credit reports. After the background check came back she was terminated from her job. Not because of poor work performance or that she had committed any crimes but because on her credit reports there showed that she had filed for bankruptcy in the past and the store concluded that this made her a bad risk for handling money.

In another case a woman was fired from a temp job that she had at a bank for 4 weeks. Her employer notified her that they had forgotten to run a credit check on her. She told them it was OK to do a credit check and told them that she had some outstanding debt from medical bills she had in 2008 when she was unemployed at the time.

They ran the credit check and when it came back she was terminated and escorted out of the building.

To see the full article check out this link:
http://www.huffingtonpost.com/2010/10/29/woman-fired-from-temp-job_n_776161.html
So as you can see knowing what is in your credit report can give you a heads up to problems that might prevent you from finding a job or keeping the one you currently have.

Here are some things you may or may not know. You have three credit reports and four credit scores.

There are three different credit bureaus, Trans Union, Equifax, and Experian. And they generate three different credit reports and three different credit scores and not everyone that you deal with may report to all three credit bureaus. So you need to know what is in all three credit reports.

You also have a score called a FICO score. This score is a major factor in how credit card companies view your credit worthiness. If you have a Wal-Mart credit card you can see your FICO score at http://walmart.com/creditlogin or if you have a Discover card you can find your FICO score on your statement or you can purchase your FICO score from the credit bureaus.

Here are some other things you may not have known. Everyone over the age of 18 has a right to get a free copy of their credit reports each year. And if you apply for credit and are turned down you have a right to see your current credit reports.

You can get copies of your credit reports each year by going to http:// www.annualcreditreport.com (see fig #1) at this site you can get copies of your reports from all three credit bureaus. The reports are totally free but if you also want to know your credit scores each individual credit bureau will charge a fee for these scores.

Fig#1

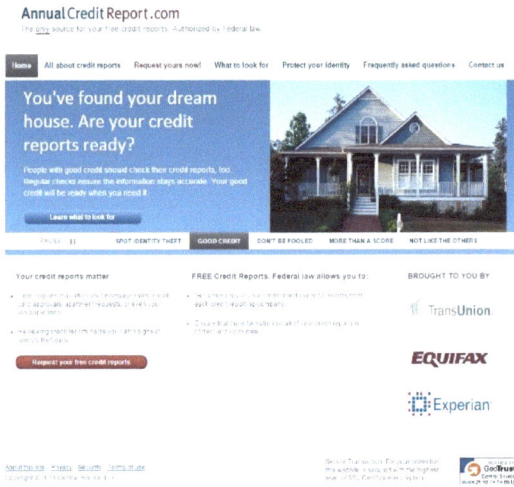

If you have never had your credit reports before getting them from the site can be a little tricky. The annualcreditreport.com site will take you to each of the credit bureau sites individually and at each site you will be asked a series of questions that may or may not be on your credit report. So if you don't already know what is and is not on your credit report then you may or may not know the answers to these questions.

If you fail to answer the questions correctly the site will not give your credit reports to you but will give you a phone number to call and/or a mailing address to send identification information.
After you make the call or send the information then you will get your credit reports by postal mail.

After you have your credit reports you need to review them for any errors such as an incorrect address, incorrect name, and any derogatory items

If you find errors on your credit reports or if you find accounts on your reports that you never opened than you may be a victim of identity theft. You can call each of the credit bureaus and try to have them fix these issues but that can be time consuming and costly. According to a report from the FTC you could spend as much as 600 hours of your time and $1500.00 out of your own pocket to try and fix an identity theft issue on your own.

If you do have incorrect items on your credit report It will be difficult to almost impossible to remove them since they will be considered pre-existing conditions and since you won't have access to all of the databases that hold your data you won't be able to make changes.

Trying to hire a credit repair service on a pre-existing condition can also be rather costly as well.

But items will drop off your credit report over time so it is important that you get a credit monitoring service so that you will be notified of any changes on your credit reports. And to get a annual copy of your credit reports each year

Now that you have your reports and have reviewed them it is time to move on to step 2

Step 2:
Getting Credit

If you have a very low credit score there aren't many credit card companies out there that will issue you a credit card. It is like the old catch 22. You have to have credit to get credit. But you have to get credit to have it.

But you do have a few options in getting a credit card. First if you have a good friend or a relative that has a good credit rating you can ask them to be a co-signer for you. The second option is to get a secure credit card from a bank or credit card company.

I do not recommend the first option. The reason I don't is because if you would default on paying the balance on the card then the card company will go after the co-signer and this could end up damaging your relationship.

I recommend the second option. Obtaining a secured credit card. The way you do this is to contact a bank or credit card company that issues secured credit cards and make and application for the card and put down a deposit from between $49.00 to 1000.00

Usually the minimum is $300.00 this goes into a savings account and works as your credit line. With this type of card if you don't go over your credit limit. And make your payments on time every month after a year your $300.00 (or what ever amount your deposit was) is refunded to you and your card converts to a regular card.

Here are some of the companies that issue secured cards
. Bank of America(see fig #2) has a card for a $300.00 deposit.

https://www.bankofamerica.com/credit-cards/products/secured-credit-card.go

Fig #2

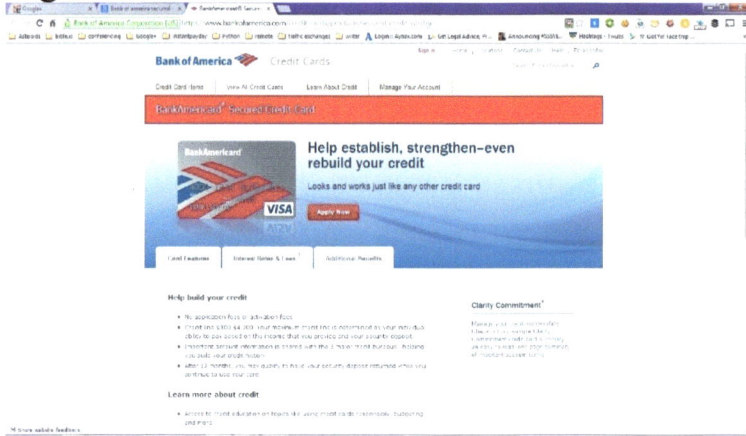

Capital One(See fig #3) issues a card for $200.00

http://www.capitalone.com/credit-cards/secured-mastercard/

Fig#3

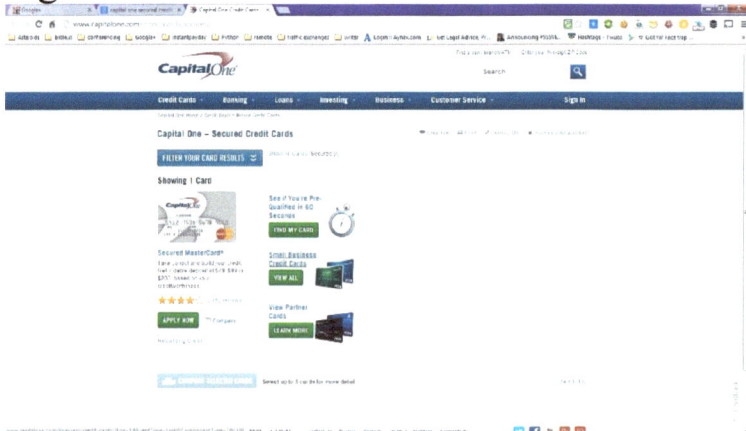

Wells Fargo(See fig #4) has one for $300.00

https://www.wellsfargo.com/credit-cards/secured

Fig#4

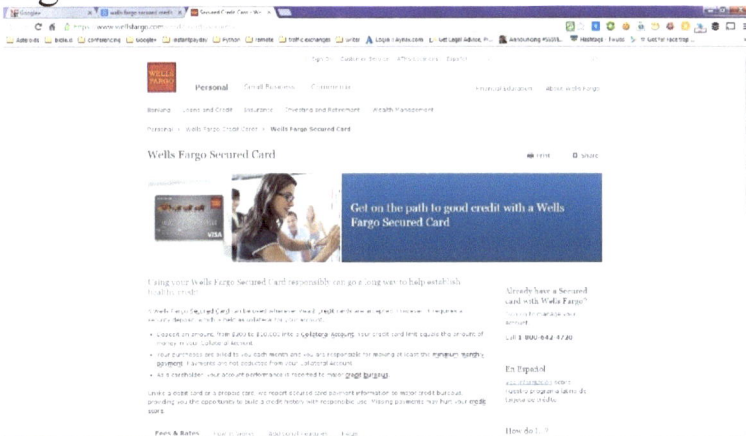

USAA for a deposit of $250.00 (see fig # 5)

https://www.usaa.com/inet/pages/banking_credit_c
ards_secured_credit_card?akredirect=true

Fig # 5

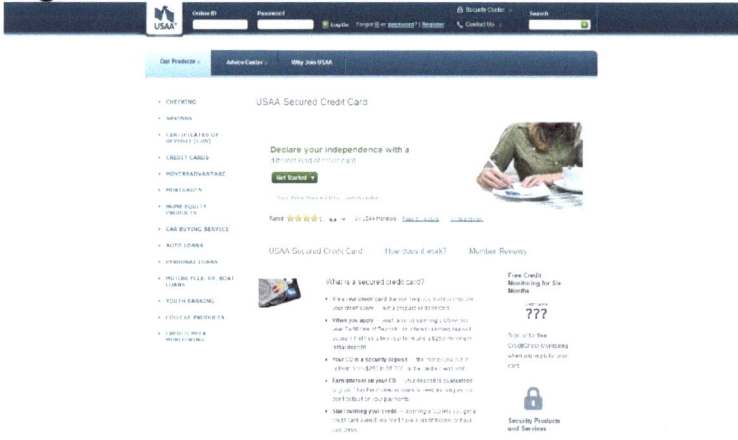

and U.S. Bank (see fig # 6)

https://www.usbank.com/credit-cards/secured-card.html

Fig #6

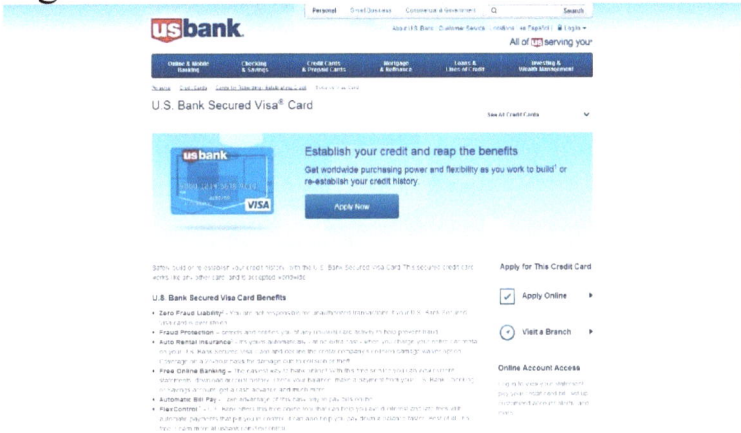

Even if you have a poor credit score you may receive credit card offers from time to time. You should be very cautious of these offers. (see fig #7)

Fig #7

Interest Rates and Interest Charges	
Annual Percentage Rate (APR) for Purchases	**36.0%**
APR for Cash Advances	36.0%
How to Avoid Paying Interest on Purchases	Your due date is at least 27 days after the close of each Billing Cycle. We will not charge you interest on Purchases if you pay your entire balance by the due date each month.
Minimum Interest Charge	If you are charged interest, the charge will be no less than $1.00.
For Credit Card Tips from the Consumer Financial Protection Bureau	To learn more about factors to consider when applying for or using a credit card, visit the website of the Consumer Financial Protection Bureau at **http://www.consumerfinance.gov/learnmore**
Fees	
Set-up and Maintenance Fees	NOTICE: Some of these set-up and maintenance fees will be assessed before you begin using your Card and will reduce the amount of credit you initially have available. Based on your initial credit limit of S500.00, your initial available credit will be only about $375.00.
•Processing Fee	**$49.00** (one-time fee)
•Annual Fee	**$125.00** for first year After that, **$49.00** annually.
•Monthly Servicing Fee	**None** for first year (introductory) After that, **$124.80** annually ($10.40 per month).
Transaction Fees •Cash Advance	Either **$6.00** or **5%** of the amount of each Cash Advance, whichever is greater.
•Foreign Currency	**3%** of each transaction amount in U.S. dollars.
Penalty Fees •Late Payment •Return Item Charge	Up to **$35.00** Up to **$35.00**

How We Will Calculate Your Balance. We use a method called "average daily balance (including new purchases)."

Right To Reject: You may still reject this plan, provided you have not used the Credit Account or paid a fee after receiving a billing statement. If you do reject the plan, you are not responsible for any fees or charges, including any Processing Fee(s) paid prior to receipt of your Account Opening Disclosures. Any such Processing Fee(s) previously paid will be refunded upon rejection of the plan.

If you ever get a credit card offer with a schedule of fees such as in fig # 7 you should avoid these like you would the plague.

As you can see the card comes with high annual percentage rate and come with a processing fee, An annual fee. And a Monthly service fee.

If you apply for one of these cards you most likely will only get a $200 - $300 dollar credit limit and these fees will be taken right off the top before you even get the card in your hand.

So by the time you actually get the card it is already almost at the credit limit. So you will be paying on fees and interest without being able to use the card.

A legitimate credit card offer will only have an annual fee of around $39 dollars. And after your credit score improves you will start to get offers that have no annual fee.

These offers can be tempting but remember that each time you apply for credit that puts a credit inquiry on your report and lower the average age of your current credit cards which could bring down your credit score.

Step 3:
Credit Monitoring

Now that you have your credit reports and your credit cards you will need to keep track of what information is being put on your credit reports.

There are a number of credit monitoring service available and I am going to tell you about a number of them that I prefer.

The first one is a call Credit Karma and can be reached at http://creditkarma.com (see fig #8)

Fig #8

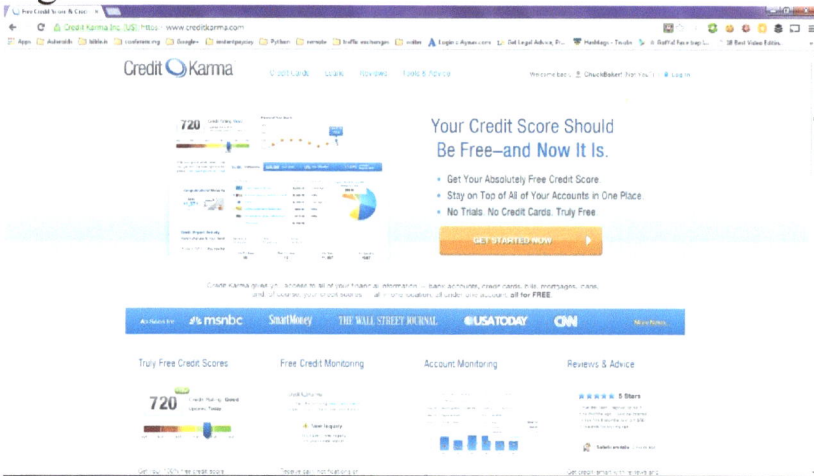

The reason why I mention this site first is because it is a free site that has a lot of features and it will give you your TransUnion credit score for free. It will also monitor your credit card and bank accounts and alert you if any thing changes and now you can even get a abbreviate version of your credit report from this site as well.

In addition it will give you a credit report card so that you know how you are doing with your credit. And it will let you know about credit offers that you might be eligible for.

The second service that I like is from Bank Of America called Privacy Assist. At http://privacyassist.bankofamerica.com (see Fig #9.)

Fig #9

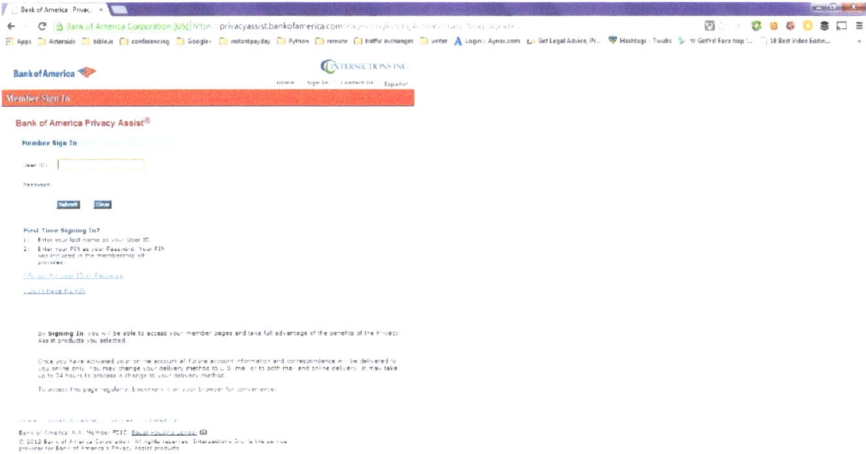

With this service you will get credit monitoring and alerts when your credit report changes and every 3 months it will give you updates on the status of your credit report.

It also gives you a credit report card and updates on your credit scores every three months. They will also monitor your bank accounts and credit card to see if any of your account numbers show up on the internet in identity theft chat rooms.

PrivacyAssist also has credit resolution services for Identity theft issues. The cost for this service is $12.99 per month.

The next credit monitoring service is Identity Theft Shield at LegalShield.com http://charlesrbaker.legalshieldassociate.com (see Fig #10)

Fig #10

With this service your experian credit report is monitored. You get a copy of your experian credit report and a copy of your TransUnion credit score. And this service has Identity Restoration Services if you become a victim of Identity theft. This service starts at a cost $14.95 per month as a stand alone service or $9.95 a month when you also purchase a standard family legal plan for $19.95 a month.

With the standard Identity Theft plan you will receive these services (see Fig #11)

Fig #11

Product Features	ID Plan	ID Premium
Member and Spouse Covered	✓	✓
Credit Report with Score and Analysis	✓	✓
Comprehensive Restoration Service by Kroll*	✓	✓
Unlimited Identity Theft Consultation	✓	✓
Safeguard for Minors℠	✓	✓
Single Bureau Credit Monitoring and Activity Alert	✓	✓

But they also have a premium plan where you not only get the services above but you also get theses services as well. (see Fig #12)

Fig #12

Triple Bureau Credit Monitoring and Activity Alert ✔

Web Watcher ✔

Daily web monitoring for unauthorized use of your Social Security Number, credit/debit card numbers and other personal information.

Public Persona ✔

Monthly monitoring of any changes to SSN or address history associated with your name

Lost Wallet Assistance** ✔

Help with canceling and replacing cards and IDs and placing fraud alerts for a lost wallet or purse.

Social Security Number Skip Trace** ✔

Social Security Number search through 34 billion public records to detect potential fraud. Identity Consultation.

Sex Offender Search** ✔

Search of sex offender databases to detect if location of sex offenders and whether a member's address has been used by a registered sex offender.

*Limitations and exclusions for Comprehensive Restoration by Kroll.

**Services will be performed upon member request.

Plans may vary depending on your state or province of residence. Go to the Plan Purchase Section for more specific details.

If you would purchase the Identity Theft premium service as a stand alone with out the legal plan it would be $29.95 per month. If it was purchased with a legal plan then it would be $19.95 per month.

Factors that influence your credit rating.

There are seven different factors that influence your credit rating. These factors are credit card utilization, payment history, age of credit history, total number is credit accounts, credit inquiries, derogatory marks, and increase in your credit limit.

These factor are grade on a scale from A to F and have varying degrees of impact on your credit score.

Credit utilization has a high impact on your credit score. For the best possible score you should only use between 1 and 20 percent of your available credit.

If you utilize more then twenty percent of your available credit each month that will make your credit score go down.

Not using your credit at all in a month's time will also make your credit score go down.

Make purchase each month with your credit up to twenty percent each month will make your credit score rise.

Your payment history has a high impact on your credit score. If you make at least your minimum payments on or before the date due that will make your credit score rise.

It is best to pay off your credit cards each month on or before the date do. This will make your credit score rise.

If you miss payment or your pay less then the minimum amount due each month this will make your credit score fall.

Average age of your credit history has a medium impact on your credit score. An average age of eight years or more will give you the best credit score. Each time you add a credit account to your credit history that will make your credit score go down.

Total number of accounts. This factor has a low impact on your credit score. Even though this factor has a low impact on your score you need to be careful about adding accounts to your credit history because doing so will also impact the average age of your credit history.

Credit inquires have a low impact on your credit score. Each time you apply for credit the bank or credit card company will access your credit report and scores. This is called a hard inquiry and these inquires can make your credit score go down.

There is another type of inquiry called a soft inquiry that does not affect your credit score.

So if you already have a low credit score it is unlikely that you would be approved for credit and applying for credit cards would only make your score go down. A hard credit inquiry can stay on your credit report for up to twelve months.

Derogatory marks on your credit report have a high impact on your credit score. If you default on your bills such as a credit card, utility bill, medical bill, or fail to pay on time any company that extends you a line of credit they can turn your account over to collections and this will show up on your credit report as a derogatory more. These should be avoided at all costs. A derogatory mark can stay on your credit report for up to 7 years.

The next factor that will impact your credit score is getting a credit line increase on an existing account. This factor isn't graded but has a high impact on your credit score. Whenever you get a credit line increase on an existing account this will make your credit score rise.

What is the difference between identity theft resolution and restoration services?

A service like what Privacy Assist provides a credit resolution service. When you are notified that there is a change in your credit report and you review the information and it isn't something you have done to make the change then you would contact Privacy Assist and let them know that you may be a victim of identity theft.

They will send you information on what to do to correct your credit report. The people you need to contact. Contact information of the credit bureaus, information on how to file police reports. Etc.

During this process keep track of expenses that you might incur such as postage for mail forms. Fees for filing reports. Hiring investigators etc.

After you feel that the matter has been taken care of you can submit your expenses to the credit resolution service and they will determine if these are valid expenses for reimbursement.

If you sign up with a credit restoration service like the one LegalShield offers when you are notified that there has been a change in your credit report and you determine that these changes were not made because of something you have done then you will call the Identity Theft Shield toll free number and let them know that you may be the victim of Identity theft. They will review your credit reports and if they determine this is the case you will have a licensed investigator assigned to your case and you will need to sign a limited power of attorney so that the investigator can access all of the information database such as your medical files your financial files. Your driving record. Your social security records. Any criminal records that might have your name or personal information connected to them.

The investigator will work to restore your record to that they were in before the recent changes accrued. This is all done by the investigator without any out of pocket expense other than your monthly membership. And the investigator will keep working your case until you tell them that the problem has been fixed.

In my opinion a credit restoration service would be the best option because you don't have to do the work to fix your credit report yourself and the only out of pocket expense would be your monthly membership fee.

Step 4:
Restoring your credit

If you already have credit but have had financial challenges and had to utilize your credit cards to their limits and your credit score has fallen don't get discouraged.

This happens to a lot of people and you can work through it. The key things to remember are to always make your credit card payments on time. If you start missing payments your APR (Annual Percentage Rate) will go up and your minimum payment amount each month with increase.

Also not paying your bills on time will put derogatory remarks on your credit report and that will drive down your credit score and derogatory remarks can stay on your credit report for up to 7 years.

When making your credit card payments you should try to make more than just the minimum payment. Only making the minimum payment each month will pay for the interest but will pay very little on the principle so it will take a very long time to pay down your cards if you are only making the minimum payment each month.

Do your best to pay off the cards with the lowest balance first. That will make one less bill that you have to pay each month, will give you a sense of accomplishment, and the money you're not spending to pay on that card can be used to pay towards the next card or things that you need.

Your instinct is to pay off the higher balances first but these balances may have higher interest rates and will have a higher minimum payment each month and this could make paying off your cards harder.

In conclusion

These are all of the steps that I have used to build my credit scores and I am sure that if you follow these steps that I have laid out you too can build or rebuild a great credit history and great credit scores.

Websites:

Wal-Mart Credit Card

http://walmart.com/creditlogin

Annual credit reports

http://www.annualcreditreport.com

CreditKarma

http://creditkarma.com

Privacy Assist

http://privacyassist.bankofamerica.com

LegalShield

http://charlesrbaker.legalshieldassociate.com

Woman fired from Job

http://www.huffingtonpost.com/2010/10/29/woman
-fired-from-temp-job_n_776161.html

Secured credit card:

Bank of America

https://www.bankofamerica.com/credit-cards/products/secured-credit-card.go

Wells Fargo

https://www.wellsfargo.com/credit-cards/secured/

Capital One

http://www.capitalone.com/credit-cards/secured-mastercard

U.S. Bank

https://www.usbank.com/credit-cards/secured-card.html

USAA

https://www.usaa.com/inet/pages/banking_credit_cards_secured_credit_card?akredirect=true